Aeons

poetry from the mist

Alexandra Henning

BookLeaf Publishing

India | USA | UK

Made with ❤ on the BookLeaf Publishing Platform
www.bookleafpub.in
www.bookleafpub.com

Dedication

To Calvin and our journey together.

Preface

In the pages of this book, I invite you into my world, into my mental space where bizarre thoughts move my pen. This collection of poems includes some brand new writing and some pulled from the catalogue of my youth. Together they bridge a gap between the parts of myself. I hope that, in reading them, you find something that resonates with your own journey.

Acknowledgements

I am deeply indebted to my family, who support me in everything I choose to do.

1. Aeon I - The Beginning

Like a freshly fallen snow,
The surface glistens.
Its seamless fabric awaits
The first impressions.

A crunch, a squeeze,
A slow compression.
Heel to toe in pristine snow
They cut my path.

Each tread upon the ground
Churns the earth beneath.
My lifescape lay splayed
By the choices I make.

Each path taken reveals
The dirt and leaves.
The snow is marred, an ugly thing,
With no way back to what had been.

2. Aeon II - The Senses

Time pours like the rain,
Drops drip down my face.
They slick, trace my veins,
And slide past with haste.

Time wafts like the smoke,
Aged ash hits my nose.
It smells of earth broken,
Yet sweet like a rose.

Time bends like the light,
Entering my eyes.
It blurs the world's sight,
Prisms refract skies.

Time tangs like the salt,
Spicy stings my tongue.
Tasting the result
Matter brought along.

Time rings like a bell,
Echoes enter ears,
End, begin, and swell,
Lasting many years.

3. Aeon III - The Whirlwind

I find the world filled.
It's blurry and I'm blind
To what I saw,
What it was,
To what I see,
What it will be.

I hold my head high,
Wind whips and I'm knocked
Down to my knees,
My core,
Down to the dirt,
My roots insert.

I grip and stand tall,
Tumult stills and I seek
The neighboring eyes,
The buds,
The fragrance nearby,
So sweet that I cry.

I breathe in and drink deeply,
Thick musk and I'm wild.
I confide and I smile,

Heart open
So wide that I bleed and slide,
Until there's nothing inside.

Am I empty?

4. Aeon IV - The Breath

I'm dancing steps in 3/4 time,
First slow, then hastening the beat.
I spin from here to there, I climb
New hands, new partners' body heat.

Within a dark, deep masquerade,
Smiling facades hide empty eyes.
Down underneath feelings cascade,
Burning within our silent lies.

I'm there stuck breathing, holding tight,
The minuet proceeds again,
Until an angel did alight
And offer hands to lift me then.

My lungs did clench and then release,
I left for good the dancing pit,
Where demon claws did rip a piece
Of my true heart now rough with grit.

5. Aeon V - The Awakening

Between the boughs, there shone a shaft of light.
It warmed the soil, a seeping heat,
The creeping moss beneath my feet did grow.
And though my chest did breath relief,
A filling, centering release,
It all went on around me -
The phlox, the thyme, the yarrow.

The rocks were crumbled, all worn down to stone.
Yet on the coolest surfaces,
Do rest slick dew, a wet to quench new life.
The vines creep with a nervousness,
As roots between the cracks finesse,
They wiggle, poke, and prod me -
Embracing all the wildlife.

And flowers spread wide open like a fan.
They strained and smelled a fragrant scent,
A pleasant sigh, swollen, and bright.
The petals soft, exposed they went
Against my skin a sweet content,
They swoon and sway upon me -
The surge was growing all night.

There rose the Sun, its warmth spread 'round the field.
A new beginning came again,
I raised my face, I felt it then and cried.
Erupting furious and when
The tenderness did calm to zen,
I felt it raw inside me -
No longer silent it lied.

6. Aeon VI - The Euphoria

Enchant me.
His smooth voice
Pouring out,
Pulling in,
Revealing my pulsing heart.

Embrace me.
His warm arms
Surrounding,
Squeezing,
Holding in the seeping parts.

Entwine me.
His deep roots
Interlacing,
Invading,
Fusing our bodies to one.

Empower me.
His whole soul
Filling up,
Fueling us,
Until our life here is done.

7. Aeon VII - The Denouement

What is this world but
Bitterly loving?

A swig of hot wine
Warms the heart and cools the senses.
A swift nebula
Consumes matter and births the stars.

I wish to deliver love unto this life
And find it reflected in kind.
No body of this world holds such promises.
No body of this universe holds such life.

Yet as the stars,
The moons,
The rocks
Return to dust,
So do I spread.
An entropic homage.

And so,
Of need and restlessness,
I love it bitterly.

8. Night Lanterns

Fireflies trickle through fields of cattails.
They tumble and topple, startle and skip,
Lighting a path through tall grass and hay bales.

The lanterns do show mice where to set sail,
Adrift a brown sea, aboard a wheat ship.
Fireflies trickle through fields of cattails.

Air thick with the pollen that we inhale,
The wind, tumultuous, lungs in a grip.
Lighting a path through tall grass and hay bales.

They follow the paths carved deep by deer trails,
Skirting the burrows with rabbits in kip.
Fireflies trickle through fields of cattails.

Then curved metal wheels squeal an iron wail,
It harries and reaves with a smoky whip.
Lighting a path through tall grass and hay bales.

The unperturbed night still seems to prevail,
As beacons return through darkness they slip.
Fireflies trickle through fields of cattails,
Lighting a path through tall grass and hay bales.

9. Night Iron

Sinuous muscle imbued with a chain,
Heavy breathing with each palpitation,
Rivers of scarlet pumped into each vein.

Kindling a fire too hard to contain,
Caressing skin for its liberation.
Sinuous muscle imbued with a chain.

With broad breaths the spirit strives to restrain,
Slighting impulse, the fringe of frustration.
Rivers of scarlet pumped into each vein.

On cotton or satin sheets I have lain,
Each time furthering this aberration.
Sinuous muscle imbued with a chain.

Driving the body until split in twain,
Embrace and satisfy delectation.
Rivers of scarlet pumped into each vein.

Locked up tight in love, in lust, in disdain,
Still as I breathe in self-condemnation.
Sinuous muscle imbued with a chain,
Rivers of scarlet pumped into each vein.

10. Night Wings

Inky wings sprout from my twin shoulder blades,
Lifting my languished core into deep flight,
A mark so deep that even time ne'er fades.

Invading the skin, bone, and blood it raids,
A demon born in the seeping black night.
Inky wings sprout from my twin shoulder blades.

Draining salt and iron from scarlet shades,
An angel flies to the city of light.
A mark so deep that even time ne'er fades.

Nothing but the wind over silver glades,
Escape from a caged life filled with spite.
Inky wings sprout from my twin shoulder blades.

Gypsies and coins play with the ace of spades,
Portents of the singular fearless plight.
A mark so deep that even time ne'er fades.

From needle to supple skin it cascades,
Final admission for soul to alight.
Inky wings sprout from my twin shoulder blades,
A mark so deep that even time ne'er fades.

11. Night Child

Lace drapes across the babe's ululation,
Tears carving his cheeks with a wrinkled path.
Mother makes one last consideration.

Dressed up with baby's breath and carnations,
Awaiting the tale of one final act.
Lace drapes across the babe's ululation,

Choking back tears through the whole duration,
The babe's intuition first feels the wrath.
Mother makes one last consideration.

With tempered and delicate frustration,
Feeling the breath and heart of an empath.
Lace drapes across the babe's ululation,

The baby writhes against in vexation,
Her soiled hands shake with the aftermath.
Mother makes one last consideration.

Bury bones in the house's foundation,
The shovel digs deep, it scoops and it packs.
Lace drapes across the babe's ululation,
Mother makes one last consideration.

12. Narcissus I - Jo Dan

The bountiful times of Spring
Spawn lovers all around.
Open your heart with caution,
And keep out such poison as
The cruelty of man.

They travel far,
Through Thespiae in Boeotia
And past the Donacon towers
To see the fountain of Narcissus.

Spring has doted on this place,
For the trees blossom,
The garden beds grow,
And grass covers the land
In a green, velvet blanket.

At last, the legendary fountain,
A shimmering pool,
Water silver-clear and bright.
Neither shepherd
Nor wild goats nor cattle
Have disturbed its still.

The surface mirrors Spring,
The surrounding trees
And the expansive blue sky.
And near the pool's edge,
A single flower yearns for a lover's gaze.

A sweet flower of white and gold.
It droops above the water
And stands for lost love
As wind winds through the willows.

The blossoms and the leaves
Live and die each season.
This white and gold flower
Returns with the most vigor.
Yet it is noted with such sorrow,
As if frozen in reflection.

13. Narcissus II - Ha First Dan

The beauty of the gardens
Are not lost on me.
The flowers are all in bloom,
And the trees are fully grown.
The willows here do not weep,
For Spring has arrived.

Yet a shadow falls
On this beauteous scene,
For nothing compares
To the visage I have seen.

I am but a humble one,
A mountain shepherd,
Come to view the splendid pool
Along my travels.

I yearn to see the beauty
That resides within
The shining, silver fountain
That shows us no lie.

I beg you to show yourself

With eyes like twin stars
And blushing as the rose
In a white snow drift.

Look deep into the water
And there you will find
Vanity and truth of soul,
Your own reflection.

I have come so far through space
To view this place
Of love, punishment, and remorse.
Please let me hold you.

14. Narcissus III - Ha Second Dan

This place is spared of ruin.
It is still the same
As it was so long ago,
Still such vividness.
Here at the legendary
Grave of Narcissus,
Greece's martyr of beauty.

The Dryads still here remain
Mourning their lost love,
All but the one called Echo
Who died of remorse.
They hide there among the trees,
Beneath the water,
And thread among the tall reeds,
Always watching.
Waiting for his return,
Tending to the white and gold flower.

They see the shepherd,
Shining beauty hidden
Beneath his common rags.
His fingers shaped as Bacchus

Might have desired.
His flowing hair glorious
Much like Apollo's.

The notorious visage
Plagues their memory,
And they ever yearn to see
Such splendor again.

15. Narcissus IV - Ha Third Dan

I will take these few steps
To the water's edge
And gaze upon the surface.
I will see what I have yearned for
These many years.
Let me embrace you.

I see his brilliance
Right in front of me.
Yet how is it that I cannot
Touch his face?

As I stare into this pool
I see Narcissus,
The most beautiful of all,
Ripple before me.
I swear with all my heart
He is not made of
The water in front of me.
Let me touch you.

Yet every time I attempt
To touch his white face,

He vanishes quickly,
Fast to disappear.

Why is it that I am cursed?
What have I done here
To deserve such punishment
And such cruelty?

Alas, this fatal image
Has won all my heart,
But I cannot press my arms
Around the form I see.

Why do you avoid me so?
You torture me so.

Oft as I strive to kiss him
He rises as if
To bring his face up fondly
And vainly to me.

How to tear my eyes away
From such brilliance?

I know not how to leave you,
And yet I must go,

For if I stay much longer,
I shall soon wither.

16. Narcissus V - Kyû Dan

Night falls upon us slowly,
Yet suddenly I see.
The round, full moon shines so brightly
It could be the day.
A white circle reflected,
The light multiplied.

Do not be fooled by the shine
Or the floating sparks,
For the willows at night weep,
The wolves do howl,
The water ripples with wind,
Reflections are lost.

This place is so beautiful,
Yet it holds pity,
And it houses repentance
For lovers' lost hearts.

Such cruelty I have endured
For not just myself,
But any star-crossed lovers
Who must also learn.

And so I do hate this place
For its deception,
Yet I cannot leave
That which I find here,
Else my heart will tear in twine,
Pain I cannot endure.

There is pain which grows each year
From frequent failure
To rekindle a lost love
Parted by much death.

Narcissus I do now know,
It is not beauty
For which you have been renowned,
But love's tragedy.

I move behind the pool, standing.
A dark tragedy of love,
Where hearts are blackened
And lost forever to gods
And to deception.

Forever will I struggle
With the incessant
Tug that pulls strong on my heart
To look fast upon

Myself reflected ever
On the river Styx.

And never shall I ferry
Across this river,
Rather always in limbo
Between lives I am.

I hate this curse and love it,
I will never leave
This river filled with the dead,
For within I see
A gray and quite sullied face
Looking back at me,
Which I can do nothing but
Love now and ever.

And so do not take my name
For thine own lovers,
And waste away in contempt
Of others who cannot
Rise to thine own quality,
For you will be cursed,
But not by the gods themselves,
By your own vanity.

17. Unwelcome I - The Rabbit Hole

In this bizarre land inhabited by creatures,
My blonde hair,
My blue eyes,
My dress and tights
Stuck out.
A sunflower in a field of deadly nightshade.

Their eyes sick with jaundice or pink eye,
Noses like beaks and snouts,
Clawed fingernails,
Hunched backs which seemed to sprout wings,
Hair growing everywhere,
Whiskers brushing the ground,
Crawling on all fours,
Screeching, squawking and growling.
My pale, smooth skin,
My manicured nails,
My perfect speech
Stuck out.
A giant among ants, miles high.

Had I known the chaos that awaited me there,
The selfishness,

The drugs,
The misleading and misdirection,
The corrupt government,
The nonsense,
I would not have entered.

Always questioned,
Never answered,
And now unwelcome.
I would not have followed the
Conniving creature down the
Rabbit hole.

Curiosity, however, won me over that
Dreamy afternoon and I ran after a stranger who
Hopped along
Dressed in a waistcoat,
Pocket watch in hand, and an
Endearing look back that whispered
Follow me.
Leaving the door wide open, he
Beckoned me across the threshold where I felt myself
Fall out of everyday reality into a
House of Mirrors.

This stranger led my
Ignorant

Innocent self to a door that would not
Open for me.

In retrospect, I should not have drank an
Unmarked bottle and eaten an
Indiscernible brownie that all but screamed
DRINK ME,
EAT ME.
They hurtled me up and down into a
Topsy-turvy,
Upside down and all around
Wrong world.
But the door then opened for me into a land run by
Blood-red hearted
Royals who constantly
Lost their heads and
Ordered their removal.
A dim-witted King who cared for little but his
Hot-headed Queen – a
Tyrant that left a
Beheaded
Bloodbath in her wake.

Creatures would turn me around,
Point me in the opposite direction and
Flee before I made sense of
What they were,

Where they were and
Who I was.

A lost identity, according to a
Hookah-smoking mushroom topper.
A maid, according to the
Whiskered ignoramus I followed
Running to his Duchess.
An unbirthday girl, according to a
Tea-addicted, insane salesman
Wearing several too-tall hats.
A dead girl, several times over, according to a
Self-righteous Queen who knows neither
How to properly run the land nor
How to play a decent
Game of croquet.

And when I finally left this
Bizarre world of
Hallucinations and
Nonsense,
I find a note by my side
Complaining of my behavior,
Politely asking for me
Never to return.

Apparently I had disrupted their

Ever-so-neatly structured
Order of
Life.

18. Unwelcome II - The Letter

Dear Giant,

I am greatly unappreciative of you
Tracking me to my
Home and stealing that which is
Not yours:
Gloves,
Fan,
Food, and
Drink.

Your uncouth behavior has
Imprisoned
My precious pepper
Duchess, barred from the
True love that is
Mine.
Barred by prison for
Boxing the Queen's ears, and
Stuck there for your
Intrusion.
Barred by betrothal with the
Duke of Knaves, a

Merciless and unworthy being who
Steals tarts and treacles, and now walks
Unscathed due to your
Interference.

For your petulance, you
Know-it-all, who
Defends his
Royal Beauty with an apparent
Lack of evidence, he is still
Free and the Duchess
Captive.

For your arrogance, I may no longer
Father a child who may rightfully be
Mine.

For your prissy wits of
Logic and
Reason, the
Trial's proceedings have gone to
Chaos.

I had placed the tarts in front of the King and the
Jurors had written all such evidence down and the
Queen had demanded a verdict and
Justice was to prevail and this mousy

Duke would be sentenced for
Stealing the tarts I so carefully arranged to be
Taken.

But you began to grow.
You pulled up you head,
You stood and you
Spouted sense into the ears of my ignorant King.
Even when he would not listen,
You grew ever more,
Your voice like a foghorn, and
Overthrew the Queen,
Bringing all to
Shambles.

The entire court,
The judge,
The jurors,
The audience,
All became a mess of
Hearts, furs, feathers,
Tea, diamonds, tails,
Roses, tarts, clubs,
Spades, fans and cards.
Until you disappeared and left a
Mess behind you.

The Duchess remains behind bars,
The Duke in front, and
I with cleaning duty.

So I will kindly ask you
Never to return again.
Sadly, you are
Unwelcome.

Sincerely,
The White Rabbit

19. Innocence I - Disbelief

Ravens caw
And fly the path
Where torches pierce the night.

Townsmen march unabashed
To iron gates,
With locks and chains,
Aiming now
To mark the veins,
Blood for blood,
A true vengeance.

An inky night
Seeps into their hearts,
Black to battle red,
Blind to bigotry.

I protest,
A voice lost among the
Shouts and jeers for retribution
Against a poor widow.

For an aging woman,
Fearing ravages of the

Hourglass upon her skin,
Senility mistaken for
Insanity.

A scapegoat hoarding
Scorned mystery and
Fatal
Accusations.

20. Innocence II - Desperation

My feet fall,
Denting the ground,
Softly chasing
Muffled shouts.

My eyes track
Ravens, pursue
Bird's eye, the
Straightest route.

My legs bound
Fallen logs, through
Foreboding screeches
Raining from the
Skies.

My body finds the
Iron wall,
Hoisting myself through a
Fault.

I race to save a
Witch, to beat the

Maddened mob's
Desperation.

21. Innocence III - Disillusionment

My breath quickens,
Straight for the door, with
Shouts of
Worry and warning
Clawing at my back.
I was not to enter this
God-forsaken dungeon, to
Endanger my
Inexperienced
Life.

I crash through a
Molded door,
Hanging lights
Flicker on a
Grand staircase.

Hanging chandeliers provide
Darkness,
Indigenous rodents
Scurry beneath my
Faulty steps.

Stairs in double time,
A breathless call - Madam -
Brings forth a
Woman.

Pounding shoes approach,
Matching
Internal heartbeats,
Masking
Staggered silence.

My gaze frozen,
Revelation,
Not on her
Sharp,
Greedy,
Grin, but her
Blood-stained
Clothes.